My Green Wife: Koji, Stefanov and Other Poets

Translated by
Chiyoko Mukai,
Mitko Vassilev
and George Marsh

My Green Wife:
Koji, Stefanov and Other Poets

Printed in a limited edition of 200 copies
of which this is number   67/200

My Green Wife:
Koji, Stefanov and Other Poets

Translated by Chiyoko Mukai, Mitko Vassilev
and George Marsh

Waning Moon Press

Some of these translations have been published in *Blithe Spirit*.
Waning Moon extends thanks to its editor.

Also available from Waning Moon Press is a series of
books of haiku written in English:
Echoes in the Heart by Michael Gunton
The Earth Drawn Inwards by Cicely Hill
Salting the Air by George Marsh
Words on the wind by James Norton

© George Marsh 1997
Cover:
Drawing by Murakami Iwao
Typography and book design:
Ian Noble
British Library Cataloguing in Publication Data.
A catalogue record for this book is available from the British Library.

ISBN: 0-9529775-4-0

Waning Moon Press
10 Gains Road, Southsea, Portsmouth PO4 OPL UK
Telephone & Facsimile 01705 793935
International +44 1705 793935

Preface

I am pleased to introuce two very little known writers to English readers. Fukunaga Koji was born in 1938 and privately educated. He started to contribute haiku to Mizuhara Shuoshi's famous haiku magazine *Ashibi* while still at school, and became an *Ashibi* prizewinner while at University. He spent his career as a teacher in a High School with other distinguished haiku poets on the staff. By 1970 he was chief editor of *Ashibi* and had started a new haiku magazine, *Oki*. He won literary prizes and critical praise for his books of collected haiku. In 1980 he died suddenly of septicemia, and two years later his widow published his third collection posthumously.

Dimitar Stefanov was born in 1932. He is a professional writer who has published poetry for adults and children, a book of essays, and many translations from Czech, Slovak and Russian. He is best known as a sonneteer, having published several collections, and is the first Bulgarian poet to publish a book of haiku, in 1988.

These English versions of Japanese poems are collaborative translations. I am not a linguist, but I worked closely with Chiyoko Mukai, who is. I started from the original text of the poem, an annotated word-list with comments on the vocabulary, a literal English translation by my collaborator or from a published source, and interpretative comments on the poem. From this information I tried to re-imagine "the haiku moment" directly into English idiom. I had intended to give myself plenty of freedom, as Christopher Logue does in his acclaimed versions of Homer (he is not a linguist either, and calls his process "adaptation"), but I found myself more and more solving problems by returning ever closer to the original's word-order - even the original's onomatopaeic sounds - and I think it is fair to say that these have turned out faithful and accurate as translations. They are certainly much more so than I had ever thought they would be, given my initial aim, which had simply been to make new poems that would work in English.

Having made my draft I would send it to Chiyoko Mukai, my Japanese collaborator, for comment. If I had strayed from the letter or spirit of the source poem I would re-write until we were happy that we were not misrepresenting the poet, and had as vigorous an English recreation as we could manage. These translations try to make fresh, as far as is possible in a new tongue and a different culture, the original poems. It is an activity a bit like an actor saying a line of Shakespeare as if he had just thought of the idea and was coining the phrase as he spoke.

For translating the Bulgarian poems of Dimitar Stefanov my collaborator was Mitko Vassilev, who provided me with his English translations and then corresponded with me over the re-draftings of our new versions.

The selections from Koji and Stefanov were made by Chiyoko Mukai and Mitko Vassilev respectively. I have made no attempt to give a representative selection of the works of Basho. Other editions are available and his work is well known. I have translated only those poems where I feel I can shed a new or different light on the poem and left out those where I have nothing to add to existing translations.

I have used a six-stressed stanza for the haiku, because it seems to my ear to have a centre of balance in English (an extra stress gives an effect of excess and a missed stress gives an effect of abruptness, curtailment). But the judgement of my ear is vindicated by scholarship too, because six stresses most accurately represent the distribution of content-words (two to a line, whether the line is five or seven syllables), and the pace of reading aloud in Japanese haiku. I am indebted to Professor Hideo Okada for this information. He has expressed the results of his researches as a theory of "foot-parallelism." He sees similarities between an English metrical "foot" and a Japanese half-line ("rhythmic segment") with one major content-word. For enthusiasts of prosody, the articles of Professor Okada can be found in *Eibungaku* (English Literature) issues of 1985 and 1986, Waseda University.

I have chosen to use an unaccented English alphabet for the Japanese names.

I gratefully acknowledge the sources of my information, which were: for the poems in the first section, by Koji, Bosha, Yuji and Shuson, Chiyoko Mukai, who kindly supplied the word-lists, her translations and her glosses on the text, which were invaluable; for the "Conjured by moonlight" section my source was the book *A Hidden Pond - Anthology of Modern Haiku* edited by Koko Kato, translated with commentary by Koko Kato and David Burleigh, published by Kadowaka Shoten in 1996, which was kindly sent to me by Mrs Koko Kato as a gift (and for this section too, Chiyoko Mukai has given me guidance on the accuracy of my readings of the Japanese, though she is not, of course, responsible for any of the clumsiness of the results); for the classic choka from the Manyoshu, Professor Hideo Okada, who sent me an article of his containing several versions of this poem in English and a commentary; for the Basho poems I used published sources, particularly Makoto Ueda's *Basho and His Interpreters*, pages from the versions of Tsunehiko Hoshino and Adrian Pinnington, kindly sent to me by Professor Tsunehiko Hoshino, and Robert Aitken's *A Zen Wave: Basho's Haiku and Zen*, kindly given to me by Carole Pook, all of which give Japanese vocabulary lists and commentaries; for the Dimitar Stefanov section the translations and notes were provided by my collaborator Mitko Vassilev. I extend sincere thanks to all the compilers of this wonderful body of poetic information.

For permission to use copyright material we are grateful to: Fukunaga Koji's publisher, Kurosaka Shoji of Araki-shuppan, who also generously sent me his edition of the works of Koji; Mrs Koko Kato for the material collected in *A Hidden Pond;* and Mr. Dimitar Stefanov for the use of his poems.

The little ink drawings are by Murakami Iwao and are used by kind permission of Kurosaka Shoji of Araki-shuppan, and the Ashibi Haiku Association.

I would like to conclude by echoing the sentiment of Mrs. Koko Kato: "I believe that there is a common ground of universal human experience upon which we can attempt to meet and understand each other, in spite of the difficulties of language."

George Marsh
Portsmouth, 1997

Translator's Note on Interpretation
In a Buddhist culture in which sitting meditation is central, words like "sit" and "wait" can indicate a special religious quality to the image. Phrases such as "coming awake," or "eyes opened" might refer to an enlightenment-like experience, and the words "nothing," "stillness," "silent" or "empty" resonate with the significance of the void, or ground of being. Basho often wore the black gown of a Zen Buddhist priest, like a crow. The paths he travelled echo with the significance of The Way (The Tao, or the religious life, expressed, in his case, through the Way of Poetry).

Contents

Shuson, Bosha, Yuji, Chiyoko

Koji

Conjured by Moonlight
- a selection of 20th. century Japanese haiku

A poem from the Manyoshu

Basho

Stefanov

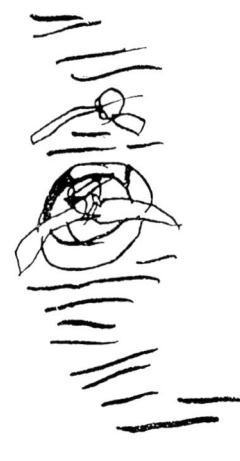

Shuson, Bosha, Yuji, Chiyoko

By Kato Shuson 1905-1993

>Opened memories
>floating in a bowl
>of clam soup

The Milky Way -
yellow quinces -
things are so real!

>He coughs
>neither of us can speak
>I cough

By Kawabata Bosha 1897-1941

On a moonlit night
a fly licks
the whole surface of the inkstone

Moonlight
fluttering on the leaves
of open-shell greens

On a stone
one dewdrop
indestructible

Scattered white petals -
the "magnolia" has vanished
so soon

By Kinoshita Yuji 1914-1965

Wild grapes -
cloud after cloud
from my native country

I keep on walking
in the heat of the sun
and so does the beetle

By Mukai Chiyoko

Deep and quiet
skyscrapers
in the winter haze

A white camellia
keeps perfect posture
after its fall

In spring's light
it's as if we know
the faces of strangers

Night in late autumn -
in the place where memories throng
crickets are singing

Anniversaries

I
My father's deathday -
I'm watching without a word
the red leaves in winter

II
My father's deathday -
those dry yellow chrysanthemums,
I want to stroke them

Koji

By Fukunaga Koji 1938-1980

> Moving in the net
> round our child's bed
> my green wife
> (Japanese mosquito nets are green)

There are things not to touch,
above all, one:
my wife's perfume bottle

> Her perfume bottle
> empty a long time now,
> mother of two

Putting on weight:
my wife's unease
and her ball of wool

Spring

(Poems written in 1979, when he moved to a new house)

A garden at last
with an infant magnolia
and a baby plum

Each morning in spring
the birds and the toaster
doing their stuff

Thrilling my garden
and house with song,
lark of the field

A pattering of rain
on the new eaves
brings me awake

All will be transformed -
I have just bedded in
a horse chestnut tree

　　　　New-planted sapling
　　　　gives
　　　　in the gusts

As summer approaches
I wait in the garden
till it fills with darkness

Summer

    A day of pootling
    around about the town -
    oleanders in flower

        Cumulothunderheads -
        I'll go and visit
        my brother's family

Grandmother's death in the rainy season

Hundreds of blooms
on the hydrangeas
drenched and dripping

Rhodedendron candlelights
stitching together
the paths through the forest

In the damp month
a white sun all day long
over the city

Summer camellias
up there this morning
in the soil this evening

Flowers of sara are white summer camel-
lias that live just one day and fall whole,
like camellias

Twirling recklessly
at the Star Festival dance
the ugly nightjar

There is a famous Japanese short story about an ugly nightjar which becomes a star after many struggles. Gilbert White describes the nightjar's twirling evening flight: "A fern-owl this evening (August 27) showed off in the most unusual and entertaining manner, by hawking round and round my great spreading oak for twenty times following, keeping mostly close to the grass, but occasionally glancing up amidst the boughs of the tree. This amusing bird was then in pursuit of some particular insect belonging to the oak; and exhibited a command of wing superior, I think, to that of the swallow itself...These peculiar birds can only be watched and observed for two hours in the twenty-four, and then in a dubious twilight, an hour after sunset, and an hour before sunrise." And Walter de la Mare has a lovely description in *Memoirs of a Midget:* "With sight strangely sharpened and powerful, I gazed tranquilly up, and supposed for a while these birds were swallows. Idly I watched them, scarcely conscious whether they were real or creatures of the imagination. Darting, swooping in the mild blaze of the moonlight, with gaping beaks and whirring wings, they swept, wavered, tumbled above their motionless pastures."

Autumn

                    The mackerel clouds,
                    scales getting smaller -
                    a good day for sprats

The twinges again -
signs in my knees
of rain in a dry month

                A day of ideas,
                bursting with fancies;
                a dozen acorns

Autumn sunset glow
on the playground
where noone plays

Attracted into
the brilliant flame -
the moth and me both

Night is so long
when I am ill -
one persimmon

Winter

Winter starlings -
a hundred-bird silence
over my head

At winter's first moves
my young trees
regress to sticks

Flakes on the chill breeze -
have they slipped through the mesh
from Heaven?

The shortest day -
a white heron looks black
against the light

Hoarfrost spikes
have sprung out overnight
like the hairs on my chin

I'm sweeping
rice-bran holly flowers -
the threat of rain

Taking the syrup -
days, perhaps weeks
think they pass

Poems written in the year of his death

> The smell of apples
> from somewhere deep in the mist
> this magical evening

> Crickets in the dark
> muttering sotto voce
> abracadabras

The locomotive headlight beam
spots the place
where apples ripen

                              Shrikes in the morning
                              and shrikes in the evening
                              with my choked voice

          How many hairs
          sprinkled around my body, hmm?
          as winter calls

My leaving hospital
celebratory drink:
still apple juice

                    The yellowed leaves
                    are the feelings of the tree
                    falling away

His last written poem:

                    My bag of bones
                    and withered chrysanthemums
                    all there is to see

Conjured by moonlight

Following the stream's current
to a single
withered reed
> Kawai Gaifu (b.1921)

In the zendo
when the coughing ceased
all sound ceased
> Satokawa Suisho (b.1927)

Swinging homeward
with my shopping: muddy leeks
the weight in the base
   Hirai Sachiko (b. 1925)

In whatever this
marvel is we call the sky
snow floats
   Hanatani Kazuko (b.1922)

Lying in the sun -
everything forgotten
even death
   Ito Michiaki (b.1935)

A hawk's nest
and nothing in the endless space
but the sun
      Hashimoto Keiji (1907-1990)

Hoot of an owl -
a pond appears,
conjured by moonlight
      Toyonaga Minoru (b. 1931)

The light has gone
leaving my heart
like winter
      Hoshino Tsubaki (b. 1930)

Face serene
after the eyes close for the last time
in faint moonlight
    Akamatsu Keiko (b. 1931)

    At the woodpecker's rapping
    leaves rush to the ground
    all through the meadows
        Mizuhara Shuoshi (1892-1981)

The light
from the other world
shows through the Milky Way
    Ishihara Yatsuka (b. 1919)

    Freezing wind
    through the whole body of the stag
    seen in its eye
        Fukuda Kineo (b. 1927)

In my Book of Complaints:
"Summer finally ends,"
and curl up in bed
   Imoto Noichi (b. 1913)

Going for water
in a snow-filled gully
I step among stars
   Okada Nichio (b. 1932)

In the pool below the falls
water's wateriness
streaming, streaming
   Yamada Reichosi (1903-1996)

Eyes gone, hearing gone
I'm groping for words
like remembering sutras
   Tomita Choji (b. 1940)

For the cuckoo's call
the lake
is a great ear
        Takaha Shugyo (b. 1930)

Angel fragments
where the butterflies swarm
in Nagasaki cathedral
        Mizuhara Shuoshi (1892-1981)

Nothing now
to hold in my hands
but the hawk owl's hoot
        Kawakami Kiseki (b. 1920)

Puking yellow stamens
at the sun -
black peonies
> Matsumoto Sumie (b. 1920)

The elephant's-ear blooms
in the mist on the marsh -
what knowledge of loneliness!
> Udo Toru (b. 1920)

For 14 centuries
the statue of the goddess
yearning for spring
> Mizuhara Shuoshi (1892-1981)

The smell of the kitchen knife
released into
spring's mist
> Ando Tsuguo (b.1919)

A lovely tree
and my black mood
changed to a butterfly
>Isogai Hekiteikan (b. 1924)

Straight onwards
comes the priest
through a storm of cherry-blossom
>Kojima Hanae (b. 1924)

On a rock in the rapids
sits
a fallen camellia
>Miura Yuzuru (b. 1930)

Looking at
my empty hands -
Easter chill
>Koko Kato (b. 1931)

White plum blossoms
are the salt of the earth -
its courage
>Nakamura Kusatao (1901-1983)

The glass panes
rattle and shake
in midwinter thunder
>Kato Shuson (1905-1993)

A choka from the Manyoshu

By Yamanoue no Okura

Thinking of my Children

The taste of melon brings my sons to mind;
Roasted chestnut moves me with memories
And the mystery of origins...
Vivid and strange they seem to me now
In the hours before dawn

And I smile to myself
With a delight
No amount of silver
Or gold or gems
Could ever inspire.

Kodomo wo Shinobu Uta, No. 802/803 of the Manyoshu

Basho

The crow sits
on a dead branch -
evening of autumn

Why flap to town?
a country crow
going to market

.

Warm hellos
and goodbyes and what happens?
Autumn in Kiso

The morning glory
with no idea what a hangover's like
blooms

Floating on the surface
of the waves of the lake
the world of summer

For a portrait of Zen Master Shrimp, the fisherman

Whitebait!
their black eyes opened
to the net of the truth

Tonight's music:
that drizzled-on dog
sleeping rough too

A whitening skull -
the freezing wind
blows through me

Snow this morning!
I study
the travellers' horses

Scooping freezing water -
my teeth go
haya ha ni hibiku!

Visiting Atsuta Shrine after its restoration

The heart's mirror
polished and clear -
snowfall like blossom

An inch or two
above dead grasses
heat waves

The petals tremble
on the yellow mountain rose -
roar of the rapids

I wish it could stay,
the face of the ugly god
fading in dawn's blossoms

        I'm ready to drop
        looking for somewhere to lay my head -
        wisteria in bloom

At Suma, the site of a great battle

The tip of the arrow
of the fisherman of Suma -
a cuckoo's call?

        Through the mist and rain
        something you cannot hide:
        the bridge of Seta

The cicadas' throbs
are so loud;
the great bell vibrating

I'll take these back
for the city slickers -
sour chestnuts

Sideways to the heath
tugging the bridle to turn
to the cuckoo-sound

My way -
noone on the road
and it's autumn, getting dark

                                          A terrible sound -
                                        the gilded helmet's
                                        trapped cricket

With what kind of voice
would the spider cry
in the autumn wind?

                                          Cats fucking -
                                        when they've done
                                        I lie in hazy moonlight

Mogami River
drags the red sun
into the sea

        The shallows -
        a crane's thighs splashed
        in cool waves

                A dragonfly, trying to -
                oops, hang on to the upside
                of a blade of grass

Deep into autumn
and this caterpillar
still not a butterfly

For a picture of a monk with his face turned away.

"This portrait depicts a man in a dream. Here I add the words of another such man talking in his sleep:"

Please turn and face me -
I'm alone too
this autumn evening

All my friends
viewing the moon -
an ugly bunch

Winter gusts
strop the crag
through a gap in the cedars

Like stroking a boil
the touch of the tip
of the willow-branch

Stefanov

From the Bulgarian of Dimitar Stefanof

On the dewy grass
to one side of the path
a single footprint

Through the woods barefooted.
Acupuncture
with pine-needles

An hour for myself.
A leaf - yellow kitten -
toddles after me

In the full pail
trembles, captured,
the full moon

This glittering morning
the snow-drift up to the door
is blue

While bees search
through the yellow dandelions
spring has come

Rainy evening -
along the tram rails
flows light

A fish tugs
the nodding rod
of a sleepy angler

A warm whiff
from the evening stones -
crickets

So many
eternal things have gone
dear little fly

The sad woods -
their eyes shedding
leaf after leaf

Summer was creaking to -
the last cricket
shut the door

                                My foot felt you
                                under the leaves, little nut -
                                sweet and ... the last one

A sleepy burdock
wags his elephant ear
fed up with the fly

                    Forest birds
                    dig in the shadows -
                    a grain is joy

Poets chew
the tender pink ham
of the sunset

This long long stem
faithfully guides you
to ... a pumpkin

In the night
a snow whale came. Pine cones crackle
in the March sun

My old boots
with a delicious crunch
on the ice crust

A lock of wool
caught on a bare hawthorn -
distant bells

Outside winter howls -
with the look of a faithful dog,
a knot on the beam

Biting sun -
across the yard
washing like broken glass

Gathered early
soaked in the sunrise -
yellow tulips

Goat tracks wrinkle
round the eye of the pool -
even you get old, time

Rain, rain, rain. Rain. Rain.
Over the bridge comes the smell
of clay, washing away

It got cold early -
the fields button up their coats
with crows

Hanging from the vine-trellis
goat-udders
with pink teats

Swimming in the river
a cloud, and on the bank
the shadow it took off

A slice of melon -
a plain dinner
fit for the gods

A woman reads a book
on the sand - the wind turns
wave after wave

Muddy boots
with autumn plumage
of speckled leaves

Like a baby elephant
stamping on the stove - soon
it will dash forward!

The storm's wet wing
swept away
even the puddles

Not so clever,
tender little snowflake, to choose
my foolish white head

Roses
smell of roses,
thank God

In bare poplars
the wind whistles
through empty nests

Bare window sills -
the geraniums
out in the April sun

                        Pieces of ice -
                        as the water-bucket slops
                        their teeth chattering

In the sand by the river
the bird feet
of the osiers

Let's see beyond
through the hole where you leak light
summer moon

The sunflower flames
burning itself
to the seeds

With just an umbrella
against the wet wind
I face the autumn